Be a Frog, a Bird, or a Tree

RACHEL CARR'S CREATIVE YOGA EXERCISES FOR CHILDREN

Photographs by Edward Kimball, Jr.
Illustrations by Don Hedin

Doubleday & Company, Inc./Garden City, New York

Be a Frog,
a Bird,
or a Tree

ISBN: 0-385-00339-0
      0-385-02358-8 Prebound
Library of Congress Catalog Card Number 72-92198

This book is for all children
who want to be healthy and strong.

I wish to thank all the girls and boys who have worked hard to be in this book. They are:

Mitra Beheshti   (pages 11, 16, 92)
Sepideh Beheshti   (page 68)
Michael Black   (pages 11, 34)
Cygalle Dias   (page 42)
Dena Fischer   (page 54)
Terry Frank   (page 79)
Brett Gelberg   (page 18)
Seth Gelberg   (page 38)
Robin Gomi   (page 20)
Kristal Hill   (page 28)
Lisa Hill   (pages 18, 26)
Melissa Hilson   (pages 34, 46 [right], 56)
Kim Hober   (pages 30, 36, 58)
Kim Larkin   (pages 32, 64)
Teddy Larkin   (page 16)
Jill Levine   (pages 12, 52)
Mark Levine   (page 48)
Robert Linde (pages 22, 72)
Randy Niederman   (pages 11, 13, 30, 54)

Tod Phillips   (pages 11, 62, 66, 74)
Roslyn Quarto   (page 11)
Elizabeth Rees   (pages 40, 46 [left], 50)
Melanie Roy   (page 32)
Jonathan Traister   (pages 11, 16, 18, 79, 92)
Shari Traister   (pages 11, 16, 18, 44)
New New Win   (pages 60, 70)
Lisa Yuen   (page 24)

Note   Our gratitude to John Kennedy for his expert handling of the developing and printing of these pictures and to Katy Hilson for her photographs on pages 34, 40, 46, 50, 56.

Introduction

Many thousands of years ago, a group of people in India invented ways to exercise based on the movements of insects, animals, and birds. They discovered that if human beings could learn to move with the lightness of a frog or a bird, or to imitate the shapes of bridges, wheels, and trees, and at the same time, stop and relax their muscles the way animals do, they could become healthy and strong. So Indians began imitating frogs and birds, bumblebees and storks, wheels and bridges, as the children in this book are doing.

These movements are called yoga exercises. They teach you balance and muscle control. And they are fun to do, as children all over the world have discovered. Those who practice the exercises regularly find that they are able to do all kinds of things better, such as running, jumping, and swimming and even riding a bicycle.

It is useful to know something about your body and how it works so that you realize all the things that it can do. For example, some people are *loose-muscled,* which means that they can do almost anything with their bodies. They find it easy to do backbends, somersaults and cartwheels. Other people are *tight-muscled* and can't move their joints easily. These people must exercise to loosen up so that they become as free with their bodies as loose-muscled people. Do you know which you are? Later on I will show you some ways to test yourself.

Whether your muscles are tight or loose, it is important to remember that you should *never force your body* to do anything you find difficult. Nature has a way of warning you. If you push yourself too far you will feel a little pain, so have patience with your body. Practice slowly, a bit each day. Before you know it you will be as quick and limber as a cat.

You will find these exercises fun from the start, but don't be discouraged if you can't do them as well as you would like to right away. If you are unable to bend your knees or your back as easily as the children in this book are doing, practice for just five minutes every day and you will soon see what a difference it makes. What you find difficult today will be easy tomorrow. All the boys and girls in this book had to practice before they could do the exercises just the way they wanted to. They worked very hard until their muscles grew stronger and became more limber.

Here are some helpful points to remember:

1. You can have more fun practicing these exercises with a friend. You can help each other as the children in these pictures are doing.

2. Some children like to do yoga exercises before supper or after school. Whatever time you choose, wait at least one hour after you have eaten before you exercise, to give your body time to digest the food.

3. Exercise on a thick rug or on folded blankets so that you won't feel the hard floor.

4. Your body should be free of heavy clothes when you exercise so that you will be able to move easily. Notice that all the children in this book are barefoot and that they are in their bathing suits. If you feel cold, put on a stretch shirt and socks, but don't wear anything heavy.

5. When you practice the balancing exercises, such as the tree, the stork, or the bumblebee, first stand on your right leg, then do the same exercise standing on your left leg. In this way you will strengthen both legs, not just one.

6. Now the last and most important point: *don't give up easily* if you find an exercise a little difficult. Just remember that it takes practice and willpower to be good at anything.

How to Begin

It's more fun when you practice with a friend so that you can help each other.

See the difference? In two weeks your body could change, as this boy's did, from the stiff pose in the left picture to the limber pose in the right picture. *The secret is to practice just five minutes a day.*

Can you touch the floor with your
head when your legs are spread apart?
If you are one of those lucky
loose-muscled people you probably can,
but lots of other people need a bit of
practice. Like this:

Put your hands on the floor close to
your legs. Now bend forward slowly
as far as you can. Count slowly up to
ten this way: one-and-two-and-three,
and so on. Do this just once each day.
Every time you practice you will be
able to reach a little lower. One day
your head will touch the floor.

If your muscles are loose you can
easily cross your legs in the *lotus pose,*
but if your knees are stiff, here is a
way to loosen them up:

Spread your legs apart. Put your right
leg over your left thigh. Hold on to
your right foot and ankle. Now press
your knee down gently and count
slowly up to ten. Remember to count:
one-and-two-and-three, and so on. Do
this once with your right leg and
once with your left leg every day. In
a week you will notice the difference.
Your knees will become loose and
limber.

Now you are ready to begin. If you follow the exercises as they
are shown here, starting with the easy ones and gradually moving on
to the more difficult ones, you will really enjoy practicing yoga.

Be a Frog, a Bird, or a Tree

16

We are birds.
We love to fly
high up
in the sky.

We can balance
on tiptoes
with our wings
stretched back.

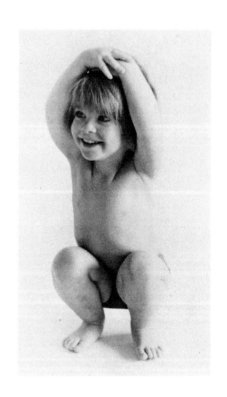

18

We are frogs.
You can hear us
croak
in a pond.

We sit on our heels
and balance
on our toes,
with our arms
around our heads.

When we are happy,
we hop about
on our toes
from place
to place.

20

I am a cat.
I love to stretch
all my muscles.
Look what I can do!

I can arch
    my
back
    with
my head
    down
and all
    fours
touching
    the
ground.

When I kneel
    on my
hands and
    legs, I
sink my back
    in and
look way
    up.

Then I lift one leg
    straight up
and turn to look at
    my foot in the air.

I am a woodchopper.
You must be strong
To be like me.

When I chop wood,
my legs are apart
and my hands are clasped
over my head.

I bend far back,
then forward and down,
and let my arms swing
between my legs, ten times.

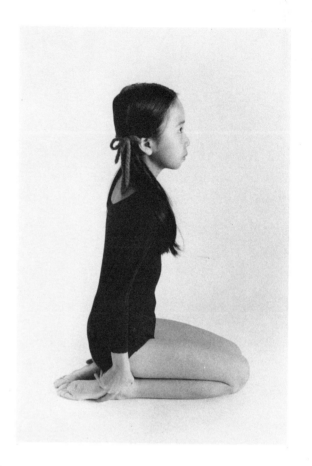

It's easy
to look
like me.
I am a hare.

I sit on my heels,
with my legs together,
and hold on to my feet.
My back is straight.

Then I bend down,
stretching my arms,
with my head
close to my knees.

I am a stork.
When I sleep,
I balance
on one leg
and bend the other one
back.

Then I tuck
my head down
and close my eyes,
with my palms
in front of my chest.

Can you balance
like me
and count
slowly
up to ten?

27

28

I am a rocking horse.
I rock back and forth,
with my body
in a ball.

I sit with my knees
close to my chest.
My arms are
around my legs.

I can rock
until my back
touches the floor,
and my feet are in the air.

Then I quickly
come forward,
with my feet
back on the floor.

I can rock this way
many times,
without letting go
of my legs.

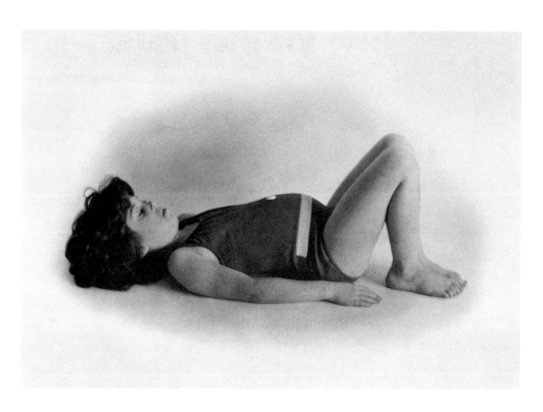

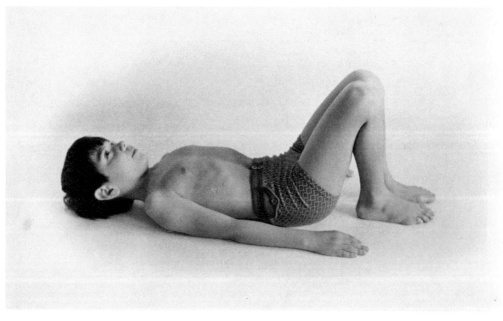

30

Guess what I am?
I can pump air
in and out of me.

I am a balloon!

When I breathe in
deeply through my nose,
I fill my body with air.
I become
round and full.

When I breathe out
through my nose,
I empty the air.
Then I become
flat and skinny.

Have you ever
seen
a tree
like me?

My left leg
is my trunk.
My right leg is
a twisted branch.

I bend my leg
so my right foot
rests on
my left leg.

My arms are
the leafy tips
of
the treetop.

I raise them
over my head,
with my fingers
touching.

Now be a tree
again,
with your left leg
as the twisted branch.

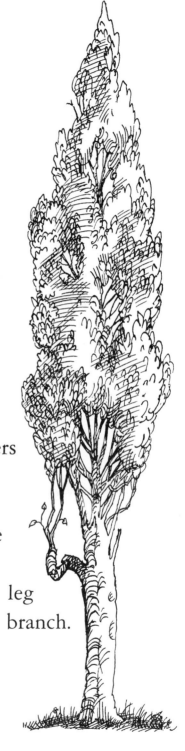

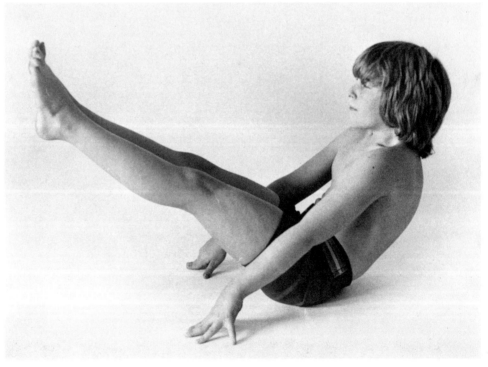

34

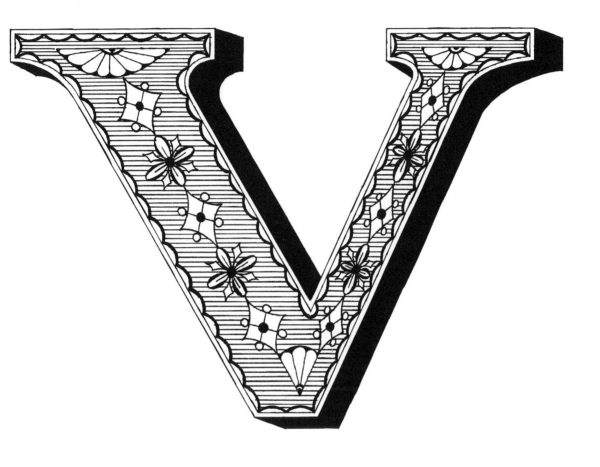

Guess what I am?

My body dips down deep.   My legs and arms
My feet and head   are straight.
are high in the air.   My hands support me.

I am the letter "V"!

I am a swallow.
I love to breathe deeply
and stretch my body.
Can you copy me?

I sit on my
heels
and raise my
arms
over my head,
with my hands
touching.

I take a deep
breath
and arch my
back
as I look up
and
stretch with all
my might.

When I am
tired,
I rest on my
heels.
My head is on
the ground,
with my arms
stretched
out.

I am a cobra.
I crawl on my
long, snaky body
in the green grass.

When I raise my head,
I arch my back
and keep the rest
of me
on the ground.

You can look
like me
if your legs and arms
are straight
and your hands down flat.

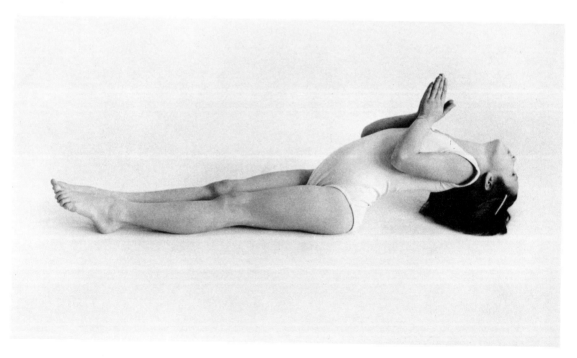

I am a fish.
My legs are my
strong tail;
my hands are
my fins.

When I float,
I put my arms
under me
to make a bridge
between
my head and back.

As I arch my back,
I slip my arms
from under me
and put my hands
together
on my chest.

Then I dream
and float away!

I am a slide.
My arms and legs
support my body
to make me strong.

I sit with my
    legs
together.
My hands
    point away
from my body.

When I raise
    myself,
my arms are
    straight
and my feet
    touch
the floor.

My head is
    back,
my body slants
downward,
perfectly
    straight.

Guess what I am?
I can travel for days
without food or water.
I live in the desert.

I am a camel!

I kneel with   Then I bend back
my legs apart.   to touch
My hands are   my feet
on my waist.   with my hands.

I am a bicycle.
My body is the frame.
My legs are the wheels.
My arms are the brakes.

When I raise my legs,
I put my hands
on my hips
to hold up my body.
It is strong and straight.

I bend my knees
and point my toes.
Then I move my legs
like the wheels
of a bicycle.

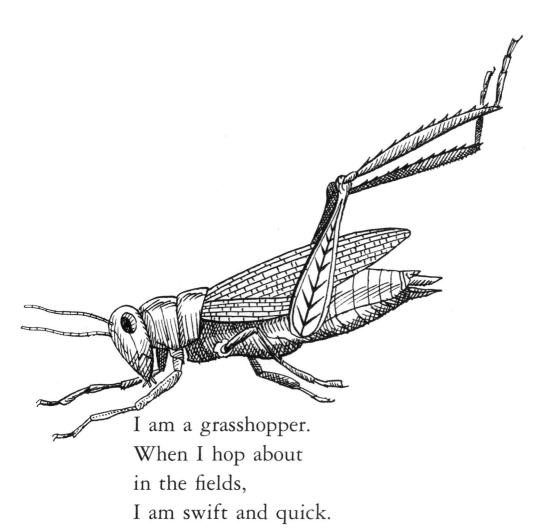

I am a grasshopper.
When I hop about
in the fields,
I am swift and quick.

This is how   To lift up my legs
I do it.   I keep my head down.
I press my fists   I take a deep breath
under me.   and up go my legs!

I am a wheelbarrow.
My arms are
the handles.
My body and legs are
the cart.

When I raise my legs
over my head,
I keep my hands flat.
My legs go up and over,
and my toes touch the ground.

Ships pass under me.
People and cars
travel over me.
I am a bridge!

To arch my
    back
I bend my
    knees,
with feet
    together
and my hands
    on my waist.

Then I raise
    myself,
with my
    elbows
close to my
    body,
to hold me up.

I slide my
    legs
forward,
with feet flat.
Now I am a
    strong
    bridge.

I am a mountain.
My legs are the base;
my arms and hands are the peak.

To make the bottom
part of me,
I cross my left leg
over my right leg
and my right leg
over my left leg.

To make the
mountaintop,
I stretch my arms
over my head,
with my fingers
touching.

Now be a different mountain,
with your right leg
over your left leg,
and your left leg
over your right leg!

I am a swimmer.
To make my muscles
strong,
I raise my arms and legs
as high as I can.

I keep them straight
so I can rock
back and forth
many times
with my head up.

58

I am a tortoise.
Once I won a race
with a hare.

When I crawl,
I spread my
    legs
far apart.

I put my arms
under my legs,
with my palms
    down.

Then I bend
    forward
until my head
touches the
    ground.

I am a swan
floating
on a lake.

I arch my back
to show my long neck.
My arms and legs
are straight.
My hands are down.

To make the tail
and wing feathers,
I bend my knees
and touch my head
to my toes.

I am a wheel.
I make things
go round and round.

I bend my knees
so my feet are
close to my body.

Then I press hard
on my palms and feet,
to lift up my body.

I bend my arms
and place my hands
near my shoulders.

My muscles become
strong and steady
when they hold me up high.

I am an archer.
I shoot with a
bow and arrow.

I bend my right leg
close to my left ear
and hold on to my big toe
to make the bow.

I reach over
with my right hand
and hold my left big toe
to make the arrow.

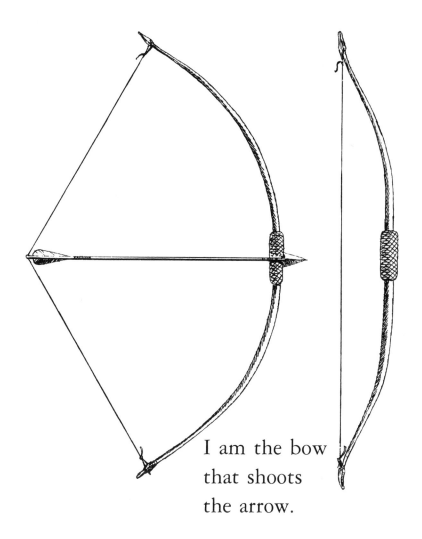

I am the bow
that shoots
the arrow.

I bend my
    knees
and hold on to
my ankles.
Then I pull
way up,
stretching.

Now my arms
    are
straight as
bowstrings,
and my head
is back.

To make my
    muscles
strong,
I rock back
    and forth,
holding on to
    my ankles.

68

Swift and straight
is my body.
I am an arrow!

I stand on
my right leg.
It is strong
and steady.

I bend my
left leg back
and hold it with
my left hand.

Then I move
forward
and stretch
my left leg out.

My right arm is
straight,
with the palm
turned up.

70

I am a bumblebee.
You can see me
flying
from flower to flower.

My body is
   straight
as an arrow.
My arms are
the wings.

I balance on
my left leg.
It is strong
   and steady.

I lift my right
   leg
straight back
and move my
   arms behind
   me
to make me
   fly.

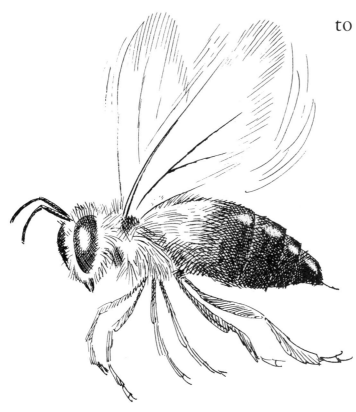

72

I am an arc.
My body is
a curve.
It's tricky to
balance like me.

I bend one leg,
with my foot flat
on the ground.
I stretch the other leg
behind me.

Then I arch my back
and raise my arms
over my head,
with my palms
touching.

I am a crow.
I balance on my elbows
to lift my feet
into the air.

This is how
I do it.

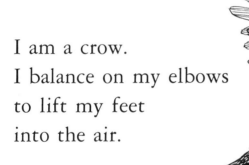

I crouch with
my legs apart.
My elbows touch
my knees.
My hands are flat
on the ground.

To lift me up
into the air,
I balance
on my toes
and press my knees
to my elbows.

Notes to Parents and Teachers

Many of us take it for granted that all healthy, active children are limber, but this is not so. When I started an experimental program teaching children creative body movements, some of them could not pass a minimum fitness test, such as bending forward to touch their toes. They had weak stomach muscles; stiff knees; tense, rounded shoulders; and little strength in the lower back.

This lack of mobility, especially in city children, is partly due to the changing life-style of our age where youngsters are chauffeured constantly, even for short distances. They run, walk, and play less today and are often quite content to sit for hours watching television. When children are deprived of balanced physical exercises, their muscles become tense and shortened, which frequently results in poor posture and other muscular disorders.

I was strongly aware that if nothing were done to improve the muscle tone of these children, many would become victims of physical disabilities that could plague them later in life. For years I had suffered from serious back ailments and stiff joints, but after following a daily routine of yoga exercises, I was able to discard the traction that I used to stretch my spine at night. Since yoga had cured me, I was convinced that anyone of any age could be helped by these beautiful, rhythmic body movements which I have adapted for children in this book.

Children are easily bored by the suspended motion required of the traditional yoga postures which adults find so beneficial and relaxing. To overcome this barrier, I encouraged children to explore the sensation of movement through mimicry, such as pretending to be a jumping frog, a flying bird, a shooting arrow, or a hopping

77

crow. They did not mind the stillness of some of the exercises when they could see themselves as a sturdy tree growing in a forest, or a strong bridge with cars traveling over it and ships passing under it.

I started this program with a handful of children in the apartment house where I live. They ranged in ages from three to ten. As the word spread that there was a lady teaching yoga to anybody who wanted to learn — and for free — many children came out of curiosity. It seemed like fun, and they asked to stay. The group soon swelled to over thirty children who came from near and far. They were of different races and nationalities.

We practiced in small groups for no more than twenty minutes three times a week, doing simple, imaginative movements to increase agility and co-ordination. The children soon discovered that they were not all able to achieve the same degree of flexibility. I explained that some children are loose-muscled and can do almost anything with their bodies, while others are tight-muscled and have to exercise to loosen up. I impressed upon the children that they could all become supple and limber if they worked hard to increase their muscle function. Being young, their bodies responded quickly. What appeared difficult to them one day was easily conquered the next. The desire to compete was so strong that they became aware of their own physical limitations, which they overcame with fierce determination.

Part of this program was also designed to teach children deep-breathing exercises which stimulate circulation, bring oxygen to the brain, and restore energy. Again, by using the power of imagination, the children became balloons and pumped away at their lungs. When they breathed in deeply, they saw themselves as balloons filled with air. They exhaled with the same controlled force to become skinny and flat, like balloons with all the air released. This visual concept appealed to their imaginations. In no time they were inventing their own deep-breathing games, as they had done with the creative body movements. When they learned to balance in the frog pose, they felt the need for continued motion and so organized frog races, croaking as they hopped with quick, well-co-ordinated movements. This led to further imaginative play. The more agile children arched their backs high up so that others

78

could crawl under them, as did this three-year-old who found great delight in exploring the unknown.

One wonderful thing about children is that they lose all self-consciousness when they become involved in what they are doing. They have an inherent need to combine sound with the rhythmic qualities of movement and so they will hiss as they slither like a snake, or chirp as they fly like a bird. They are able to concentrate so completely on being the snake or the bird that they become one with it, and without realizing this, they are using the key muscle groups of their bodies. Because children use movement as a vehicle for creative expression, this provides a necessary release for the hyperactive child.

In the course of teaching, I discovered another quality about children: they are often the best teachers of other children. When a six-year-old boy was struggling with the pose of the archer, his older sister came to the rescue.

"It's really very easy," she assured him. "Just think of your left leg as a long telephone wire. It is connected to your right hand. The telephone is your left foot, and you listen with your right ear."

What may have seemed a complicated explanation to an adult was just the right clue for the little boy. He immediately mastered the archer.

In less than three months the children were quite at ease with the thirty different body movements shown in this book, some of which require ultimate physical control. They could also do backbends, cartwheels, leg splits, and headstands. Even the children with a limited sense of physical rhythm improved considerably. The experiments were more successful than I had dreamed they would be. Yoga soon became an intrinsic part of the lives of the children.

They talked about it constantly, and I have often heard some of them say: "First I'll do my homework, then my yoga." They worked even harder when they learned that they were to be selected to pose for the exercises in this book.

Since normal children responded so well to this creative concept of physical exercise, I was eager to explore the capabilities of the handicapped. I embarked on such a program at the School for Language and Hearing Impaired Children, a public school in Manhattan. I had three classes, each of which consisted of about twelve children. Even with the help of teachers who understood the individual problems of each child, the challenge was overwhelming. I used pictures of children in the poses of the frog, mountain, fish, bicycle, and bird, with drawings to convey these images as they appear in life. The children caught on fast. Even though their attention spans were limited, they became excited. Those who could talk made every conceivable sound while imitating the postures of animals, birds, insects, and objects. The hard-of-hearing children would lip-read and watch the others so as not to miss anything.

Drama in action was commonplace because of the immense hurdles these children face daily in life. In less than four months there was a remarkable breakthrough in some psychological barriers. For example, when a seven-year-old girl who had never uttered an intelligible word before discovered that she was able to touch her toes to her head in the pose of the swan, she made every attempt through gestures to attract my attention. In desperation she shouted, "LOOK! LOOK!" This spontaneous desire to speak startled her as much as it did the teachers and me.

I encouraged the more able children to help those with less physical control, and they did this with a tremendous understanding of the other children's disabilities. When one boy in the group found the pose of the tree too confusing, tears sprang to his eyes. His jerky, unco-ordinated movements frustrated him. Rushing to his aid was a lithe youngster whose hearing and speech were so impaired that he communicated only in sign language. He gently led his friend to a wall for support, then moved the boy's trembling limbs into the pose of the tree. The triumph brought spontaneous applause from the entire group.

The children all showed a capacity to retain about twenty-five different body movements they had learned over a period of six months, in slow, repetitive stages. The imagery concepts helped develop their powers of retention and were reflected in other facets of their lives. They gained confidence and became in closer touch with themselves. In their free drawings they often expressed various forms of body movements they had learned with me. One eight-year-old boy drew an ocean of fishes. At the bottom was a large fish lying peacefully in the yoga pose. It was the only fish he had colored.

When the children were relaxed and happy they showed a sense of humor. Once during a moment of chaos I called out sternly: "Is this a fish market?"

The ones who understood promptly lay on their backs in the pose of the fish, eyes closed and faces smiling. The rest followed as they caught on. A voice soon spoke up, breaking the silence.

"There are ten fish in this fish market." It was an emotionally disturbed boy of nine who spoke. He had a string of phobias, and one of them was expressed by his determination not to remove his shoes while exercising because of his fear of dirt. But that day he lay on the mat in his stocking feet with all the other children. His shoes were neatly placed within reach.

Perhaps the best way to explain the success of this program is to quote a letter I received from the Assistant Principal of the School for Language and Hearing Impaired Children, Mrs. Georgianna Khatib:

Our classroom teachers and physical education instructors alike have been enthusiastic in their response to your program, for they see the pleasure of the children during each session and their gradually increasing competence from week to week. There have been some quite remarkable changes in performance by individual children and a generally impressive development by the groups with which you've worked. The philosophy of your program seems quite sound and is consistent with, though different from physical activities done in the physical education classes in school. Your approach and expertise have provided experiences in movement which are unique and obviously enjoyable for the children, and we've been particularly aware of the amount and natural quality of the verbal expression of the children as they engage in their analogous play.

As a parent or teacher you may ask how such a program can continue to appeal to children. It can, with the help of the parent or teacher who is willing to guide the child with gentle persuasion and encouragement by varying the daily exercises to maintain the spirit of fun and excitement. In this way the first rush of interest the child may have will be continually nourished.

I am convinced that all children, regardless of their physical or mental capabilities, respond instinctively to these creative body movements and that the benefits to be gained from them extend far beyond mere physical fitness.

HOW TO USE THIS BOOK

If you wish to teach these exercises to a child, he will probably enjoy them more if he does them with a friend. Most children enjoy group learning. It inspires them to compete and teaches them sportsmanship. If you plan to teach the exercises to a number of children, the group should be only as large as the parent or teacher can manage, which is usually about eight to ten children, preferably of about the same age. If the group is larger, there should be adequate supervision so that each child will have the necessary individual help.

Children's maximum attention spans differ according to age. Here are some guidelines:

20–25 minutes for children from ages 7–10

10–15 minutes for children from ages 5–6

5 minutes for children from ages 3–4

Here is one way to liven up the process of teaching these exercises. Ask the children to form a circle with their exercise mats, or on a large carpeted surface. Select one child at a time to enter the circle and demonstrate the pose, as the other children follow. Teach no more than two new exercises at a time, and repeat the earlier ones to improve flexibility and muscular control. The more familiar children become with the various body movements, the more enjoyment they will get out of them.

If these exercises are presented as games, children find them exciting and often become quite inventive in making up their own variations. For example, you might arrange a contest involving the balancing exercises such as the tree, crow, arrow, and bumblebee, which require concentration and muscular control. The child who holds a pose the longest would be the winner.

Pantomime is a natural outgrowth of yoga exercises. Ask one child to stand before the group and pantomime an exercise. The rest should guess what it is. Or, have two children pantomime a skit, such as a cat watching a bird, a tortoise in a race with a hare, a bow and an arrow, or an archer and a swan.

PANTOMIMING CAN BE FUN

The Archer and the Swan

The Woodchopper and the Tree

The Cat and the Bird

The Tortoise and the Hare

The Cobra and the Crow

84

The Bow and the Arrow

Flight of the Bumblebee and the Grasshopper

Swimmer under a Bridge

You will find that as you teach the exercises you will begin to develop your own ideas to stimulate interest. The children will do the same. The Notes on the Exercises section will help you observe the correct postures as well as the individual benefits of these rhythmic body movements.

HOW TO PLAY THE GAME OF RELAXATION

All children will benefit by the game of relaxation, particularly those who are high-strung and overactive. Some children can be made to relax easily, while others will fidget and become irritable. But with continued direction in teaching them to let go completely, they eventually become receptive and will not resist the period of rest. This should come after a session of exercises. The instruction in relaxation should be slow and emphatic for about five minutes.

Have the children lie on their backs, with eyes closed, and their arms and legs loosely outstretched. Dim bright lights to induce a quiet atmosphere. With a soft voice relax them in this way:

Close your eyes. It is time to put your body to sleep for a few minutes. When you wake up you will feel fresh and strong again. Be quiet and still so all your muscles can relax. First put your feet to sleep. Don't wiggle your toes. Let each toe relax by itself. Then put your legs to sleep by keeping them very still. Don't move your arms or move your fingers. Soon they will feel loose and free. Keep your body very still. Breathe in deeply, and let your tummy fill up with air like a balloon. Now breathe out slowly, and let your tummy sink in like a balloon without air. Breathe in again. Fill your tummy once more with air, then slowly breathe out once more as your tummy sinks in. Now lie very still. No whispering. No giggling. No sighing. No moving. Everyone is going to sleep. Fast asleep . . . fast asleep . . . fast asleep.

Notes on the Exercises

1. THE BIRD   Improves posture and balance; strengthens feet and ankles. Can be turned into a game of flying birds. Children under five are unable to maintain the correct pose, as the six-year-old on the right, but they enjoy being birds ready to take off. (See pages 16–17.)

2. THE FROG   Improves posture and balance; limbers knees, strengthens feet and ankles. Can be turned into a game of jumping frogs. Most children under four find it easier to maintain balance with their feet flat on the floor rather than balancing on their toes. (See pages 18–19.)

3. THE CAT   Provides complete body stretch, especially for hamstring muscles. In the first pose, feet and palms are flat on floor, the head is down. The back is arched high. In the second pose, the back sinks in, and the head is up. When the leg is raised in

the third pose, the head is turned toward the toes. Alternate right and left leg for this movement. (See pages 20–21.)

4. THE WOODCHOPPER Stretches spinal column and releases excess energy when up-and-down movements are repeated vigorously about six times. Fingers are interlocked throughout exercise. (See pages 22–23.)

5. THE HARE Gives spinal column stretch; sends fresh supply of blood to brain when head is lowered close to knees; hands are fully stretched holding on to ankles. Buttocks are raised. (See pages 24–25.)

6. THE STORK Exercise for balance and concentration. Eyes are closed when balance is held steady. Alternate right and left legs. (See pages 26–27.)

7. THE ROCKING HORSE Good for tight-muscled and overweight children. Repeated vigorous movements, rocking back and forth about ten times, will flex spinal column and hip musculature. Arms are clasped around legs throughout exercise. (See pages 28–29.)

8. THE BALLOON   Key to
deep-breathing exercise stressing use
of diaphragm: *Inhale and inflate
abdomen; exhale and draw in abdomen.*
Breathing is through nostrils only.
Stress relaxation of body; children tend
to tense up when first learning to
breathe deeply. (See pages 30–31.)

9. THE TREE   Exercise for balance,
concentration, and spinal-column
stretch. Note how sole of one foot
rests on inner thigh of other leg. Arms
are stretched upward with fingertips
touching. This can be turned into a
counting game of balance. If the child
fixes his eyes on a stationary object,
it helps to steady balance and improves
concentration. Alternate right and
left leg. (See pages 32–33.)

10. THE LETTER "V"   Abdominal
and hip strengthening; muscular
emphasis is on hips and thighs. Neck
and shoulders should not be tensed.
Back is slightly curved to maintain
balance. Palms are flat and close to
thighs. (See pages 34–35.)

11. THE SWALLOW   Complete
body stretch is emphasized in the
stretching upward and reclining
movements. (See pages 36–37.)

12. THE COBRA   Spinal-column stretch; strengthens lower back. Palms are close to chest when head is raised in a slow, snakelike movement until arms are fully stretched and head is back. The same snakelike movements are used when the body is slowly lowered to the floor. (See pages 38–39.)

13. THE FISH   Spinal-column stretch; strengthens lower back. Palms are flat under buttocks. When chest is arched and head is centered on the floor, the elbows support the body. Then arms slip away from body and are placed over chest with palms touching. (See pages 40–41.)

14. THE SLIDE   Strengthen arms, legs, and back. Body is on a plane; buttocks must not sag. Hands and feet are firmly on floor. Neck is relaxed. (See pages 42–43.)

15. THE CAMEL   Spinal-column stretch. When bending back, hands touch heels. Legs are apart. Neck is relaxed. If a child tends to stiffen his shoulders and neck, this can be prevented by holding him so that he feels the sensation of bending backward. (See pages 44–45.)

16. THE BICYCLE   Strengthens lower back and hip musculature. Children with weak back muscles are unable to raise their legs in a vertical position. Let them practice by rolling backward to gain momentum so that they can raise their legs. Elbows rest firmly on the floor to support the hips. Once balance is secure, children enjoy rotating their legs like the wheels of a bicycle. This makes a good counting game. (See pages 46–47.)

17. THE GRASSHOPPER Strengthens lower back and hip musculature. Head remains on floor when legs are raised. Knees are straight. Hands are made into fists and placed under groin; this helps to raise legs. (See pages 48–49.)

18. THE WHEELBARROW Stretches hamstring and spinal column. Tight-muscled children should practice raising and lowering their legs just above the head to stretch the spine. When legs reach over the head, toes should touch floor. Arms do not move, palms remain flat on floor. (See pages 50–51.)

19. THE BRIDGE   Strengthens arms, legs, and spinal column. When body is raised, legs slide forward and together, with feet flat on floor. Elbows support arch by bringing them close to the body. Head rests comfortably. Children who find this exercise difficult should be helped by lifting up the spine so arch can be felt as legs slide forward. (See pages 52–53.)

20. THE MOUNTAIN   Limbers knees and stretches spinal column. Tight-muscled children should practice the limbering exercises on pages 11–13. Three- and four-year-olds should start with the simplified versions of the Mountain. (Left) Legs fold one over the other with arms stretched above head, palms touching. (Right) Ankles cross in kneeling pose with arms stretched above head, palms touching. Note how older child has fingertips touching rather than the palms. (See pages 54–55.)

21. THE SWIMMER   Strengthens abdomen and spinal column; also good all-round tone-up of body and limbs. To increase strengthening of muscles, have children rock back and forth with head up. Arms and legs are close together. (See pages 56–57.)

22. THE TORTOISE   Stretches hamstring and spinal musculature; strengthens abdomen. Difficult for tight-muscled children. Should be practiced gradually. (See pages 58–59.)

23. THE SWAN   Strengthens abdomen and stretches spinal column. Hands are flat on floor; arms straight and close to body; legs together. Neck is relaxed and stretched back, with toes reaching up. Takes practice for tight-muscled children before toes and head meet. (See pages 60–61.)

24. THE WHEEL   Stretches hip and spinal musculature; strengthens abdomen and limbs. Children with weak back muscles need help by supporting spine so they can feel muscles in action. (See pages 62–63.)

25. THE ARCHER   Stretches hamstring and spinal musculature. Hands grasp only big toes and not entire feet. A way to remember this exercise is that the *right hand grasps the left big toe; left hand grasps the right big toe.* Outstretched arm is over the bent leg. Alternate right and left leg. Note how arms and legs are fully stretched and taut, as body leans slightly forward. (See pages 64–65.)

26. THE BOW Strengthens abdomen, arms, legs, and spinal column. Children who are unable to raise their legs off the floor need a little help. Grasp their upper arms to give them a boost. With practice this exercise can be turned into a rocking game. Arms should be taut as bowstrings. (See pages 66–67.)

Exercises for Children Seven and Up

27. THE ARROW Complete body stretch; a balancing exercise and a lesson in concentration. Eye is fixed on an object to steady balance. Children learn this exercise quickly if they use the support of a table or chair to develop muscular control. As body moves forward, bent leg is stretched back. Supporting leg is firm and straight. Alternate right and left leg. (See pages 68–69.)

28. THE BUMBLEBEE Complete body stretch; a balancing exercise and a lesson in concentration. Follow same teaching principles as in the Arrow to maintain steady balance. Body is on a plane to give feeling of swiftness of flight. Supporting leg is firm and steady. Alternate right and left leg. To help center the mind on this

exercise, have children make the buzzing sound of the bee as they balance. (See pages 70–71.)

29. THE ARC Complete body stretch; also a balancing exercise. One leg sweeps backward without bending knee; other leg is bent and close to body. Arms stretch back with palms touching. Alternate right and left leg. Tight-muscled children need help by supporting their spine as they arch back. (See pages 72–73.)

30. THE CROW Strengthens entire body musculature; also a balancing exercise. Should be practiced on a cushioned surface to prevent hard falls forward, just as a safety measure. Elbows rest firmly against inner part of knees with body crouched in a balancing pose. By pressing down on the palms, this will help to raise the legs. Requires practice before muscular control is developed. Children inherently throw their legs up when practicing this exercise. (See pages 74–75.)

How the Photographs Were Taken for This Book

Photographing the children was an experience in itself. I wanted them to be just as free and happy in the pictures as they were when they practiced yoga with me. There was only one way to achieve this. The pictures had to be taken in an environment where the children were comfortable. So with the help of my husband, Edward Kimball, we converted our living room into a temporary studio every Saturday morning. The source of natural sunlight from our river view made the setting ideal. Our "studio" also became an emergency clinic for cuts and bruises, stomach-aches, and emotional catastrophes that never failed to occur during our photographing sessions.

Every Saturday was turned into a festive occasion for the children. They felt they were coming to a party. Frequently they brought along little brothers and sisters and unexpected friends from the neighborhood to show off their own students who were able to perform these yoga exercises with the same surprising vigor and enthusiasm that they, as self-appointed teachers, had.

Since the children were at ease with my husband, I urged him to try his hand at photography. He did, and these are the results of his first pictures selected from a range of 700 he had taken during the six-month period. He succeeded in distracting the children from the camera by joking and talking to them while he captured them in these beguiling poses.